Rolling Right Along

By Sue Bursztynski

NELSON
CENGAGE Learning

Australia • Brazil • Japan • Korea • Mexico • Singapore • Spain • United Kingdom • United States

NELSON
CENGAGE Learning

Rolling Right Along

Text: Sue Bursztynski
Illustrations: Julian Bruere
Editor: Fleur Godding, Purr Communications
Design: James Lowe

Acknowledgements

The author and publisher would like to acknowledge permission to reproduce material from the following sources: Photographs by AAP Image, p. 27 bottom; akg2, pp. 21, 22; APL/Corbis/Bettmann, p. 14/ Giedeon/Mendel, p. 18 centre; Index Stock Imagery, cover inset/ pp. 12, 23, 28 top right; Mary Evans Online, pp. 23 top, 27 top; Newspix, pp. 17 bottom, 30 left; photolibrary.com, cover, pp. 4 top, 4 centre, 4 bottom, 5 left, 13 top, 13 bottom, 19 top, 19 bottom, 29 left, 29 top right, 29 bottom right, 30 centre right; Photos.com, pp. 13 centre, 17 top, 28 bottom right; Photo Edit Inc., pp. 30 top right, 30 bottom centre; Picture-desk.com/Kobal Collection, p. 18 bottom; Science Photo Library, pp. 11 left, 11 right.

Text © 2004 Cengage Learning Australia Pty Limited
Illustrations © 2004 Cengage Learning Australia Pty Limited

For product information and technology assistance,
in Australia call 1300 790 853;
in New Zealand call 0508 635 766

For permission to use material from this text or product,
please email **aust.permissions@cengage.com**

ISBN 978 0 17 011658 9
ISBN 978 0 17 011655 8 (set)

Cengage Learning Australia
Level 7, 80 Dorcas Street
South Melbourne, Victoria Australia 3205

Cengage Learning New Zealand
Unit 4B Rosedale Office Park
331 Rosedale Road, Albany, North Shore NZ 0632

For learning solutions, visit **cengage.com.au**

Printed in China by 1010 Printing International Ltd
7 8 9 13 12

Contents

Wheels
within Wheels

When you hear the word 'wheel', what do you think of? Cars, bikes and other forms of transport? The wheel has played a very important part in the history of transport since it was invented in Mesopotamia in about 3500 **BCE**. It has made all the difference in being able to reach places quickly and has influenced what goods can be produced and sold. It even helped determine who won wars. Train wheels made a huge difference in the 19th century.

Did you know?

The South and Central American civilisations found that the wheel just wasn't practical and they managed well without it. The Egyptians had the wheel and they stopped using it when they decided that pack-carrying animals suited them better for transport.

THE SPINNING JENNY.

But the wheel means much more than transport. It has been a vital part of our lives for thousands of years. Improvements in the wheel helped people find new ways of doing things.

When more pottery was needed for bigger populations, for example, a quicker way was found to produce it – the pottery wheel. For centuries, women spun thread for cloth-weaving on sticks called spindles. When more thread was needed, the spinning-wheel came along, and it must have been a very important achievement: think of all the fairy-tales in which a spinning-wheel plays a part! An improvement in that wheel, the spinning jenny, completely changed the lifestyles of many country people, who had to go to town and work in factories.

Let's take a short tour through the history of this simple but important invention. Roll up, roll up!

Origins
of the Wheel

Imagine a world with no wheels. There are no roads, and therefore no cars or even carts. No one turns pottery on a wheel or spins thread on a spinning-wheel. And then, one day, somone has a bright idea and the world is changed forever.

Letter to the King of Uruk

To Gilgamesh, Lord of Uruk, beloved of the gods,

Greetings!

As Your Majesty ordered, I have examined the new device, brought to the city market this morning by a farmer who used it to carry his goods for sale.

He calls it a 'cart' and the wooden discs which move it 'wheels'. As he explained to me, he had split a log, made planks and cut three slices for each 'wheel'. These are hammered together and attached to rods called 'axles', then pegs hold the wheels in place underneath the box. The wheels and axles turn and move the cart on its way, pulled by an ox. The farmer said the ox was already pulling his plough, so why not his cart?

It is indeed impressive, Sire. The merchants to whom I spoke had no interest in the idea, since they have pack animals, but I believe we can make use of this idea in war, perhaps using swift donkeys rather than oxen. We would need to build artificial tracks on which to run them if we are to use them properly, but if the cart were lighter and some way could be devised to lighten the wheel, it would be highly effective. The warrior could shoot arrows or throw spears while a comrade drove the donkeys. It would also increase the speed with which our armies could travel, giving us a huge advantage over our enemies.

I am bringing the farmer and his cart to the palace to show you this afternoon, but will send this tablet ahead with a swift messenger.

Your Majesty's loyal servant,

General Enkidu

Mesopotamian wheels

The wheel is thought to have been invented in Mesopotamia, in what is now Iraq, in about 3500 BCE. Unfortunately, wood doesn't last that long, so we don't have any original wheels left, but there are ancient pictures of Sumerian **chariots** with heavy-looking wooden wheels. There were solid disc wheels in Northern countries, but the Mesopotamian ones were made up of three pieces. Later, the heavy wooden wheels were replaced by lighter metal ones with spokes.

As with a lot of modern technology, war was the reason for improving the wheel. Better wheels meant that chariots could be lighter and could travel more quickly. Metal (bronze) tyres around the rims kept them from wearing out. But metalworking technology had to be improved first.

Imagine what it must have been like to be an enemy of the first Sumerian king who had these travel devices and to see them rushing towards you on the battlefield!

Bicycles

When German Baron von Drais began riding a wheeled machine around his gardens for exercise in 1817, he wasn't the first – a Frenchman had built one in 1790 – but his was unique because it was steerable.

The 'hobbyhorse' or 'Draisienne' was nothing like your modern mountain bike with its multiple speeds and gears. It was wooden and had no pedals. It was more like a scooter you could ride. Still, it was very popular in the early 1800s.

Bicycles continued to develop, as people experimented. In 1860, a French hobbyhorse repair man, Pierre Michaud, was fixing a bicycle when he got the bright idea of attaching pedals to it. It still wasn't much like the bicycles we know, but riders didn't have to push any more. It was nicknamed 'boneshaker' because the awful roads of the time made it very uncomfortable to ride.

Tyres became metal, then solid rubber. Then in 1888, a Scottish vet, John Boyd Dunlop, made some air-filled tyres for his young son's tricycle. His experiment made a huge difference to the way wheels could now be used.

John Dunlop

Dunlop and a bicycle with air-filled tyres

The most famous nineteenth century bike is the 'penny-farthing', which was popular with young men. It had a large and a small wheel. The trouble was, it was hard to mount and was very unsteady, and it was not a good bike for women in long dresses. Also it was expensive, because it had to be made especially for your leg length. It cost an ordinary worker six months' pay. Other kinds of bikes had to be developed, till everybody could ride one.

So next time you go on your paper round or ride to school, remember how far the bicycle has come in nearly two centuries!

Did you know?

There are over 8 million bicycles in Beijing, the capital of China, alone. In Denmark, bikes are used for 20–30 per cent of daily city travel. In Asia, bicycle-powered **rickshaws** are used for 10–20 per cent of carrying goods. Early motorbikes had pedals that worked in the same way as a bicycle.

Ferris Wheel

'The wild man with wheels in his head': George Ferris and his invention

New Attraction at World's Fair

By Samuel Smith

Chicago, June 16, 1893

Engineer George Ferris has built the main attraction of the World's Fair which opens in a few days, a fairground ride to be named after him – the 'Ferris wheel'.

'It all began a couple of years ago when we attended an engineers' banquet,' explained Mr Ferris's wife, Margaret, who was beautifully dressed in black and gold for the occasion. 'They were already planning an event to celebrate the four-hundredth anniversary of Columbus's landing in America. After all, if the French could have their Paris Exhibition to celebrate the centenary of their Revolution, why couldn't we celebrate *our* big event? Someone complained that while the French had the **Eiffel Tower** at their Exhibition, we had nothing to outdo it. "And what's so special about the Eiffel Tower, anyway?" my husband argued, "It's just a bridge turned sideways. We can do better than that, surely."'

312m

80m

15

Mr Ferris had been doodling on a table napkin, a drawing of a merry-go-round carousel, which he turned on its side. Then he took his napkin up to the main table and showed it to the men there, suggesting that they could use cars instead of horses. They became very excited at the idea.

However, it nearly hadn't happened. Mrs Ferris said, 'The organisers of the fair agreed to give George the concession in the fair grounds until they realised exactly what he had in mind. Then they nearly cancelled it. They said he was some sort of crazy wild man with wheels in his head! But finally, it was all organised and they started building.'

The wheel is an impressive 250 feet in **diameter** and has a **circumference** of 825 feet, with a 45-foot-long axle, the largest single piece of forged metal in the world. There are thirty-six cars, each of which can hold sixty people, and they revolve, powered by two engines, each of a thousand **horsepower**. The car goes slowly up until the entire city can be seen from a height of 266 feet in the air.

The view is spectacular as all forty members of the invited party gasped with pleasure. Mrs Ferris opened a bottle of champagne, climbed up on a chair and drank a toast to her husband and the success of his wheel.

The wheel opens to the public, at fifty cents a ride, on Thursday and will be there for the whole of the fair.

Did you know?

There are two modern giant Ferris wheels: one at the Prater amusement park in Vienna and London's Millennium Wheel. The Prater park has had a wheel since 1897, not long after the original one was built in Chicago. It is 200 feet high and can carry hundreds of people. Its cars are big enough to host large functions. The London wheel, also known as 'The London Eye', was built in 1999 and has become a major tourist attraction.

Pottery Wheels

Before the wheel, potters used other methods, such as resting the base of the pot on a flat bowl and turning that. This method is still used in some countries and still works. It just wasn't fast enough, for once villages became towns, trade expanded and more pottery was needed. There had to be a faster way of turning pots around as they were sculpted.

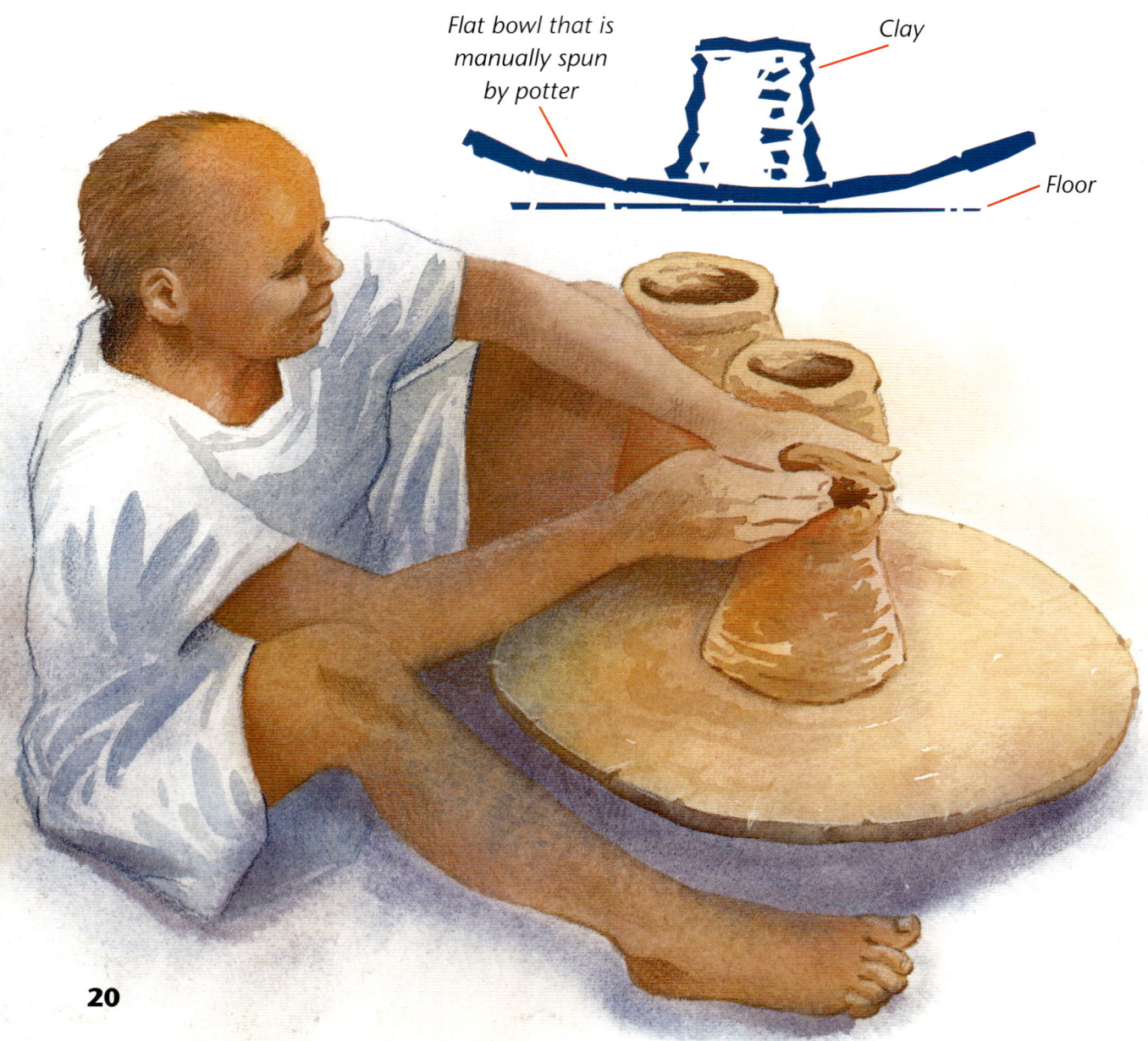

Flat bowl that is manually spun by potter

Clay

Floor

The first actual pictures of pottery wheels are Egyptian wall paintings from about 2400 BCE. They were pictured on stands, which made them easier to turn. Like pottery wheels everywhere, they were simple wooden discs, used to help potters turn around the pots they were making from long coils of clay, so they could get at the other side as they pinched the clay flat and smoothed it out. For a very long time, pottery wheels were used only to speed up coil pottery.

With a lot of experimentation, wheels became easier to turn, but it was much later that the ancient Greeks came up with a design known as the kick-wheel, where the foot could be used to turn it from below. In Europe, by the 16th century, potters were using a high **turntable** with a large wheel underneath for the feet to move. This method continued until the 19th century.

Most modern wheels are electric and potters use the method known as 'throwing', which involves placing clay in the middle and working on it while it spins. However, some modern potters enjoy using the earlier method of spinning the wheel by hand and foot. Pots can be thrown on these wheels as long as the wheel is spinning. The wheel has to be kicked again as soon as it begins to spin slower.

It is amazing how much people have been able to do with a little imagination and a simple disc!

Did you know?

Potters were highly respected in ancient Egypt, where there was even a Festival of the Potter's Wheel. It was believed that the ram-headed god, Khnum, created humans on his pottery wheel.

Chapter 5

Spinning Wheels

*Mr James Hargreaves speaks:
an exclusive interview with our
correspondent in London, 1768.*

I spoke to James Hargreaves, inventor of a new machine, the spinning jenny, at his home in Blackburn. Mr Hargreaves won the weaving industry competition to create a faster means of spinning thread for use in the exciting new cloth factories.

Q. Mr Hargreaves, thank you for your time and congratulations on finally building the machine you designed some fourteen years ago.

A. Thank you, sir, but I'm not sure it's such a good thing. The local spinners have been attacking my home in protest. My family and I have had to move to Nottingham.

Q. Dear me, isn't this rather over-reacting?

A. For me, it is. I understand the anger of the people who have been spinning at home. This machine only needs one person to run it and does the work eight people did before. These people will now be out of work. Some will get jobs in the factories, others will not. But they must understand that the weaving industry needs more thread. They just can't produce it quickly enough at home.

Q. Could you describe the spinning jenny for our readers?

A. Really, it's only a treadle-powered spinning-wheel that can operate several spindles. One person can make them all turn at once, producing more thread than on a normal wheel.

Q. Would you like to take us through a history of spinning until the present day and suggest some possible improvements in the future?

A. Certainly. Most spinning until the early **Middle Ages** was done with spindles and distaffs. These were two sticks. One, the distaff, held wool, which you spun onto the other, the spindle. The weight on the bottom of the spindle is called the whorl. It makes spinning easier. A skilled spindle spinner can do as well as one using a wheel.

Here in England, we had the great wheel, called a walking-wheel, which we first started using in the fourteenth century, though it was being used in France and other parts of Europe in the thirteenth century. It was turned with one hand and the thread drawn out with the other. The worker had to step forward to draw out the thread each time – not very comfortable! Some English spinners 'walked' about thirty miles a week.

The Saxony wheel is turned by a treadle so that the spinner can sit, and work with freed hands. It has a spindle. This was invented in the fifteenth century. I understand it is very popular in the American colonies.

The future? I don't know. Perhaps a spinning jenny that controls more spindles? I hear somebody is already designing one called the spinning mule.

Good luck, Mr Hargreaves!

Did you know?

The Indian flag has a spinning-wheel on it! This is the charkha, which is still used in many parts of Asia. It has spokes, but no rim, only ropes around the edges. The spinner sits on the ground and turns the handle, spinning the thread on to a spindle. The flag's design was the idea of independence leader Gandhi (pictured below), who had his own charkha.

The **Wheel** in the **Modern World**

Take a walk down the street. Look around you. Wheeled cars, bikes and scooters whiz past. Your wind-up watch has wheels in it. When you put on your in-line skates or step on to your skateboard, think of the wheels that are helping you enjoy yourself. When you play your CDs and tapes, they spin – like wheels. Inside the players are more wheels. At the supermarket, wheeled trolleys make carrying groceries easier.

The **turbines** that power **hydroelectric plants**, planes and ships are wheels. They came from the water-wheels that used the pushing-power of streams or waterfalls to help grind flour. There were wheels in the first televisions and calculators, and gears – little toothed wheels – are still a vital part of machinery.

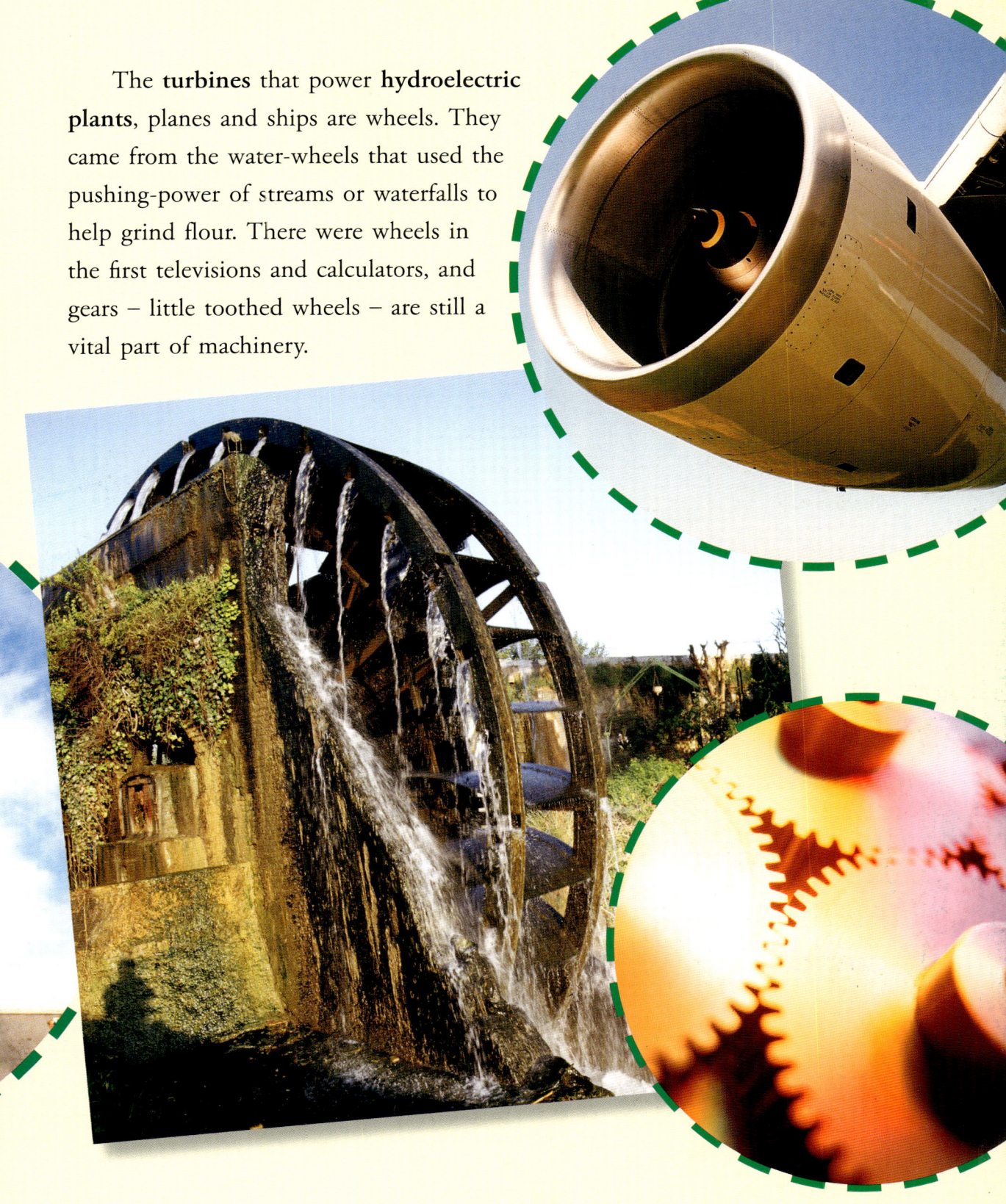

Those who can't walk may use wheelchairs. They are often motorised now (but still on wheels). The first wheelchair was built in the sixteenth century for King Philip II of Spain.

People make pottery on modern wheels and spin for enjoyment, though modern spinning-wheels have bobbins for winding thread instead of spindles.

Did you know?

In the Middle Ages, the wheel was a symbol of how life can change for people. There were many paintings of the Wheel of Fortune, showing people reaching the top (success), while others plunged to the bottom, in despair. Everyone, it was believed, was tied to this 'lucky' wheel and would reach the top or bottom sooner or later.

We speak of 'the wheels of industry' or 'the wheels of justice'. Someone who works hard is putting her 'shoulder to the wheel' or 'nose to the grindstone' (a wheel that sharpens tools).

The wheel is still with us and will be for a long time to come.

Glossary

BCE
Abbreviation meaning 'before the common era', used instead of BC (before Christ).

Chariot
A light, two-wheeled transport that was pulled by horses or, in Mesopotamia, by donkeys in ancient times. It was used in battle and for racing.

Circumference
The distance around the edge of a circle.

Diameter
The distance across a circle.

Eiffel Tower
Cast-iron tower in Paris, a tourist attraction. It was built for the Paris World Fair of 1889.

Horsepower
A unit of power, used to describe how powerful an engine is. One horsepower is equal to 550 pounds (250 kg) being lifted (or pulled) one foot in a second.

Hydroelectric plant
A place where electricity is generated using the pushing power of water.

Middle Ages
A period of time from around the year 1000 to the year 1500.

Rickshaw
A small, two-wheeled carriage pulled by a person, either on foot or riding a bicycle.

Turbine
A type of motor powered by gas or water. It is made up of wheels.

Turntable
A rotating disc or platform. Turntables can be used as a bench for making pottery, and can spin a CD or a record that plays music.

Further Reading

Bender, Lionel, *Invention*, Collins (Eyewitness Guide), 1991

Brown, Julie and Robert, *Inventions*, adapted from Michael Holt's *Inventions*, Belitha Press, 1990

Locke, Ian, *The Wheel and How it Changed the World*, Simon and Schuster Young Books, 1993

Lord, Trevor, *Amazing Bikes*, Dorling Kindersley, 1992

Roberts, Derek, *The Invention of Bicycles and Motorcycles*, Usborne, 1975